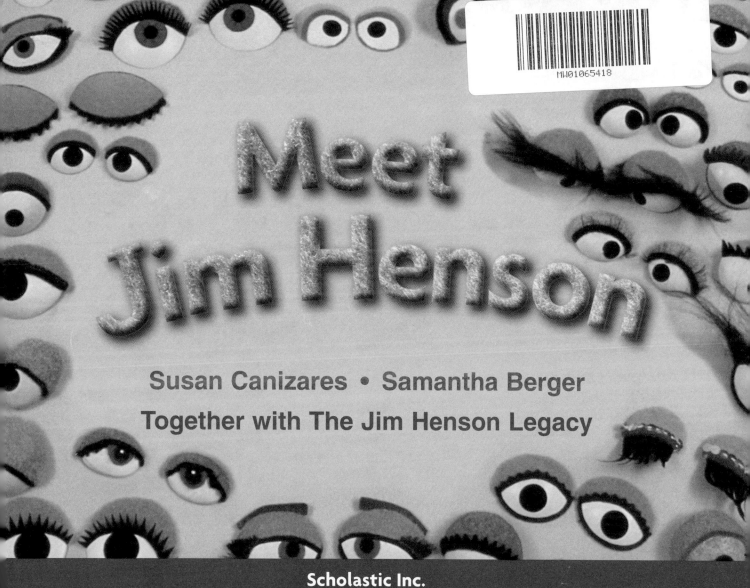

Meet Jim Henson

Susan Canizares • Samantha Berger
Together with The Jim Henson Legacy

Scholastic Inc.
New York • Toronto • London • Auckland • Sydney

Acknowledgments

Literacy Specialist: Linda Cornwell

Social Studies Consultant: Barbara Schubert, Ph.D.

Design: Silver Editions

Photo Research: The Jim Henson Company

Endnotes: Elizabeth Scholl

Original photos by John E Barrett, David Dagley, Nancy Moran, Marcia Reed, Edward T. Sahlin, Richard Termine, and others.
Original artwork by Michael K. Frith, Donald Sahlin, and Jim Henson.

1   2   3   4   5   6   7   8   9   10   08   03   02   01   00   99   98

Meet Jim Henson . . .

and a small green frog.

Kermit!

Jim and his friends

made friends for Kermit.

They made a fuzzy brown dog.

Rowlf!

They made a pretty pink pig.

Miss Piggy!

They made two best friends.

Bert and Ernie!

You know Jim already!

Meet Jim Henson

Jim Henson was born on September 24, 1936. Growing up in Leland, Mississippi, Jim enjoyed drawing, painting, and cartooning. He also loved fishing and spending time outdoors.

Another thing Jim liked to do was listen to the radio. Television had only recently been invented, and not many families had one at the time. One radio show Jim particularly liked was called *Edgar Bergen and Charlie McCarthy*. The show starred a man named Edgar Bergen, who was a ventriloquist, a person who can talk out loud without moving his lips. Bergen's partner, Charlie McCarthy, was actually a puppet, but to Jim and lots of others, Charlie seemed like a real person.

When Jim was young, he and his family moved to Maryland. Jim asked his parents to buy a television for their new house. Television was new and exciting, and Jim loved watching it. One of his favorite television shows was *Kukla, Fran, and Ollie*. Kukla and Ollie were puppets and their partner, Fran, was a real person.

From watching and listening to these shows, Jim grew to like puppets. He liked them so much, in fact, that he joined a puppet club in high school. He also drew pictures of puppets, and even began to build puppets to look like his pictures.

It was during this time that people at a television station in Washington, D.C., were looking for someone to be a puppeteer, a person who works with or performs with puppets, on one of their shows. Using some of the puppets he had built, Jim tried out for the show and got the job! The show only lasted several weeks before it was

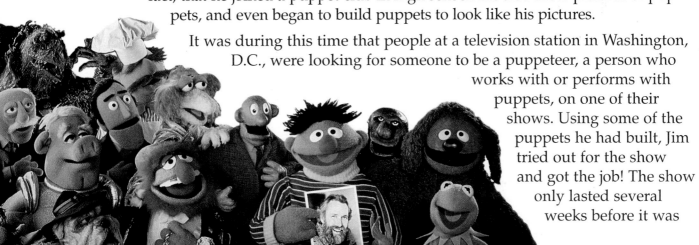

canceled, but some people from another TV station saw it, liked what they saw, and hired Jim to work as a puppeteer on one of their shows. Before long, Jim was asked to create his own TV show with puppets. The year was 1955 and the show was called *Sam and Friends*. It starred, among others, a little green character named Kermit, a puppet Jim had made out of an old green coat of his mother's and a Ping-Pong ball cut in half for the eyes.

Jim enjoyed performing puppet characters, especially Kermit. It wasn't long before Jim thought of a name for his puppets—MUPPETS. The word is a combination of the words "puppets" and "marionettes."

In 1969, Jim was asked to create a whole new group of Muppet characters for a children's television show called *Sesame Street*. Kermit visited the show often and soon became a regular guest. *Sesame Street* and its well-known characters Bert, Ernie, Big Bird, and the rest of the group quickly became very popular. The show went on to win many awards, including the best television show for children. Thirty years later, it is seen by children in many different countries all over the world.

Jim was happy about the success of *Sesame Street*, but he still wanted to use his Muppets to entertain families and people of all ages. By this time, he had many people working with him, people who loved the Muppets, too. There were writers and producers, puppet builders and puppeteers, and many others. They all worked together to create a new show for families called *The Muppet Show*. This show, too, was very popular and seen all over the world. And, of course, Kermit was on *The Muppet Show*, only now he was the star.

Jim and his friends continued to make new puppets for several movies and new television shows, including *Fraggle Rock, The Muppet Movie, The Great Muppet Caper, The Dark Crystal,* and *Labyrinth*, where he began experimenting with high-technology puppets run by computers.

Jim Henson believed that working can be fun and exciting. He hoped that, through his television shows and movies, people could learn how to work well together, be great friends, and help one another. For Jim, life was to be enjoyed, and his enjoyment of it brought joy to many people throughout the world.